ROSEMARY

ROSEMARY

INTRODUCTION BY KATE WHITEMAN

southwater

This edition is published by Southwater

Southwater is an imprint of
Anness Publishing Limited
Hermes House
88–89 Blackfriars Road
London SE1 8HA
tel. 020 7401 2077
fax 020 7633 9499

Distributed in the UK by
The Manning Partnership
251–253 London Road East
Batheaston
Bath BA1 7RL
tel. 01225 852 727
fax 01225 852 852

Distributed in the USA by
Anness Publishing Inc.
27 West 20th Street
Suite 504
New York
NY 10011
tel. 212 807 6739
fax 212 807 6813

Distributed in Australia by
Sandstone Publishing
Unit 1
360 Norton Street
Leichhardt
New South Wales 2040
tel. 02 9560 7888
fax 02 9560 7488

1 3 5 7 9 10 8 6 4 2

Publisher Joanna Lorenz
Senior Cookery Editor Linda Fraser
Project Editor Anne Hildyard
Designer Bill Mason
Illustration Anna Koska

Photographers Karl Adamson, Edward Allwright, James Duncan, John Freeman, Michelle Garrett and Patrick McLeavey
Recipes Catherine Atkinson, Jacqueline Clark, Joanna Farrow, Christine France, Shirley Gill, Christine Ingram, Maggie Pannell, Liz Trigg and Steven Wheeler
Food for photography Jacqueline Clark, Joanna Farrow, Katherine Hawins and Jane Stevenson
Stylists Madeleine Brehaut, Hilary Guy, Blake Minton and Kirsty Rawlings

For all recipes, quantities are given in both metric and imperial measures and, where appropriate, measures are also given in standard cups and spoons. Follow one set, but not a mixture, because they are not interchangeable.

Previously published as *Cooking with Rosemary*

Contents

$\mathscr{I}$NTRODUCTION

An intensely aromatic shrub native to Mediterranean countries, rosemary grows happily in sandy, rocky places with scanty soil. It takes its name from the Latin *Rosmarinus*, rose of the sea, and can often be found growing on the sides of cliffs or near the shore. Rosemary is also widely cultivated in gardens, where it is valued for its pleasant aroma, culinary and medicinal uses and for the protection it gives against insect pests.

There are countless picturesque legends associated with rosemary and the belief in its mystic powers persisted for centuries. It was the symbol of friendship and the custom was for friends of a dead person to throw sprays of rosemary "for remembrance" into the grave. Sprays were also strewn before a bride.

Rosemary has always been a favourite with gypsies. They used to peddle a preparation made from flowering rosemary sprigs, known as Queen of Hungary's Water. It was much valued by women as a cure-all and beauty tonic. Gypsies also kept a sprig in their vans to protect against evil forces and tucked it under a child's pillow to prevent nightmares. The Arabs used dried powdered rosemary as an antiseptic for the umbilical cord of new-born babies. The Spanish also believed in rosemary's antiseptic powers; they pounded it with salt to make a paste which they then applied to wounds.

The small, needle-like leaves are dark green, tough and very aromatic. Their volatile oils stimulate the secretion of digestive juices and so arouse the appetite. Whole leaves are too spiky for comfort so they need to be very finely chopped or, if left on a sprig, removed before serving. The blue-mauve flowers are said to have originally been white, but there is a legend that the Virgin Mary rested beside a rosemary bush on her flight into Egypt and threw her robe over it; the flowers turned blue in her honour. They look pretty scattered over strawberries or poached pears.

Rosemary combines well with meat, particularly fatty varieties, such as lamb and pork. It is also good mixed with lemon zest in fish dishes, stuffings and tomato-based sauces. A small sprig adds a subtle flavour to milk used for desserts and to syrups for fruit salads.

This book begins with advice on how to grow, prepare and store rosemary. The first chapter shows how rosemary adds pungency to fish and seafood dishes. The chapters on meat and poultry will have you smacking your lips in anticipation. We go on to show how rosemary's powerful presence adds depth to vegetarian and vegetable dishes, breads, pasta and pizza. The final chapter offers a delightful and surprising selection of vinegars, preserves and drinks.

Types of Rosemary

STANDARD BUSH

Rosemary bushes (*Rosmarinus officinalis*) tend to grow quite vigorously, quickly reaching a height of 1.5 metres/5 feet when planted in an open border. However, they also flourish in containers, a method of cultivation that provides greater control, and are well suited to planting in a raised bed. 'Tuscan Blue' and 'Majorca Pink' are ideal varieties for the smaller garden or patio, as they have neat growth, bright, ornamental flowers and are excellent for all purposes, including cooking. The variety known as var. *albiflorus* has white flowers. There are also some varieties with gold or silver stripes on the leaves, but these are less hardy than common green rosemary. These tend to be grown for ornamental rather than culinary purposes.

'SILVER SPIRES'

An old variety with mid-blue flowers and fine silvery leaves, this is more usually grown for its appearance rather than for culinary or medicinal use.

'MISS JESSOPP'S UPRIGHT'

Also known as 'Fastigiatus', this is a tall, hardy upright variety with lighter green leaves than normal and pale blue flowers.

PROSTRATE

The prostrate version (*Rosmarinus officinalis* 'Prostratus') has fine leaves and bright blue flowers. Like other trailing varieties, it is tender and needs heat in winter in order to survive. It grows well in rock gardens.

SEMI-PROSTRATE

While more vigorous in habit than prostrate varieties, semi-prostrate rosemary tends to be less rampant than standard bushes. The best-known semi-prostrate variety is 'Severn Sea'.

DRIED ROSEMARY

Rosemary is one of the very few herbs whose leaves keep their flavour well when they have been dried. Store them in an airtight, dark glass jar away from heat and light. However, as all varieties of rosemary are evergreen, fresh leaves are available all year.

WHOLE STEMS

Woody rosemary stems create a wonderful aroma when burned on the barbecue or on an open fire. They are traditionally burned when Easter lamb is spit-roasted after the Lenten fast in eastern Orthodox countries.

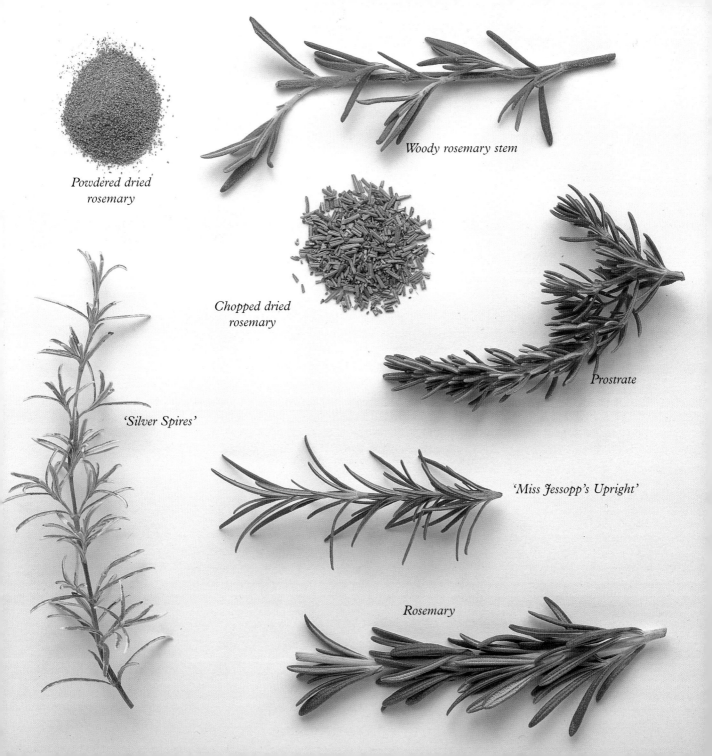

Powdered dried
rosemary

Woody rosemary stem

Chopped dried
rosemary

'Silver Spires'

Prostrate

'Miss Jessopp's Upright'

Rosemary

$\mathscr{B}$ASIC $\mathscr{T}$ECHNIQUES

PREPARING ROSEMARY

Rub your fingers down the woody stem two or three times to strip off all the leaves.

To chop the leaves very finely, use a very sharp knife with a curved blade or a mezzaluna.

Tender leaves from the tip of a young rosemary shoot can simply be snipped off with scissors.

COOK'S TIPS

• *Rosemary with poultry* When grilling chicken, tuck small sprigs of rosemary under the skin.

• *Rosemary oil* Put a large sprig of rosemary in a bottle of olive oil and leave for two weeks before using to allow the flavour to develop.

• *Rosemary stuffing* A tablespoon of finely chopped rosemary combined with breadcrumbs, lemon zest, egg and seasoning makes a delicious stuffing for poultry or breast of lamb.

• *Rosemary with olives* Store black olives in a screw-top container with plenty of chopped rosemary. Add enough olive oil to cover. The olives will keep for several weeks.

• *Rosemary sugar* Put a sprig of rosemary in a jar of sugar and use in baking and desserts.

RECIPE IDEAS

Grated courgettes with rosemary Put 3–4 grated courgettes in a pan with salt, pepper, finely chopped rosemary and a knob of butter. Cover and cook over medium heat for 5 minutes, shaking the pan occasionally. Stir in cream and heat through.

Rosemary and roasted beetroot Roast peeled beetroot with olive oil, chilli flakes and a few sprigs of young rosemary.

Plum compote with rosemary For a delicious compote, cook halved plums in a sugar syrup flavoured with orange peel and a sprig of rosemary.

Rosemary sauce Dice 1 onion and 1 apple and fry in 30ml/2 tbsp butter. Stir 15ml/1 tbsp cornflour into 300ml/½ pint/1¼ cups light stock, add to the pan, stir in 75ml/5 tbsp tomato purée and bring to the boil. Sieve and reheat with sugar and finely chopped rosemary.

ROSEMARY SHORTBREAD

Serves 4

Pound 30ml/2 tbsp finely chopped rosemary with 50g/2oz/¼ cup caster sugar. Sift 100g/4oz/1 cup plain flour and 50g/2oz/½ cup rice flour into a bowl. Mix in the rosemary sugar and 2.5ml/½ tsp vanilla essence. Rub in 100g/4oz/½ cup butter and knead into a ball. Place on a board sprinkled with rice flour and press into a 20cm/8in diameter circle. Place on a greased baking sheet and prick all over with a fork. Pinch the edges with your fingers. Bake in a preheated oven at 180°C/350°F/Gas 4 for 20–30 minutes until pale golden. Mark into eight segments and leave to cool completely on the baking sheet.

Fish and Seafood

Combined with other robust ingredients, such as wine and tomatoes, rosemary adds richness to sauces and marinades for Mediterranean-style fish and seafood dishes.

SALMON WITH ROSEMARY MARINADE

Make good use of fresh rosemary in this marinade, which is ideal for barbecued salmon.

Serves 4

several fresh rosemary sprigs
90ml/6 tbsp olive oil
45ml/3 tbsp tarragon vinegar
1 garlic clove, crushed
2 spring onions, chopped
4 salmon steaks
salt and ground black pepper
lemon wedges and mixed salad
*   leaves, to serve*

COOK'S TIP

Include other chopped fresh herbs in the marinade if you wish. Chervil, thyme, parsley, sage, oregano and chives are all suitable. This marinade is also good with meat and poultry, including veal, pork, lamb and chicken.

Discard any coarse stalks or damaged leaves from the rosemary, then chop the leaves very finely. Mix with the oil, vinegar, garlic, spring onions and salt and pepper.

Place the fish in a bowl and pour over the rosemary marinade. Cover and leave in a cool place for 4–6 hours.

Brush the fish with the marinade and cook under a preheated hot grill or over a barbecue, turning occasionally, until it is tender. Baste the fish with the marinade while it cooks. Serve with lemon wedges and salad leaves.

ROSEMARY MULLET IN BANANA LEAVES

The exceptionally sweet and rich flavour of red mullet is enhanced by the aroma of rosemary, and banana leaves help to seal in the juices of this firm-textured fish.

Serves 4

8 small red mullet or kingfish, about 175g/6oz each

8 fresh rosemary sprigs, plus extra to garnish

banana leaves or wax paper

30ml/2 tbsp olive oil

salt and ground black pepper

Preheat the oven to 220°C/425°F/Gas 7.

Wash, scale and gut the fish or ask your fishmonger to do this for you. Lay a rosemary sprig inside the cavity of each fish. Cut a piece of banana leaf or a sheet of wax paper large enough to wrap each fish.

Drizzle the mullet with a little olive oil and season well. Wrap each fish securely in the banana leaves or wax paper. Place the parcels on a baking sheet, seam side down. Bake in the oven for about 12 minutes, until cooked through and tender. Unwrap the parcels to serve and garnish with more fresh rosemary sprigs.

COOK'S TIP
There are two varieties of red mullet available. The best is actually called golden mullet.

ROSEMARY BAKED FISH

This North African dish, evoking all the colour and rich tastes of Mediterranean cuisine, is served with an unusual and delicious rosemary-flavoured sauce.

Serves 4

1 whole white fish, about
   1.1kg/2½lb, scaled and cleaned
10ml/2 tsp coriander seeds
4 garlic cloves, sliced
10ml/2 tsp harissa sauce
90ml/6 tbsp olive oil
6 plum tomatoes, sliced
1 mild onion, sliced
3 preserved lemons or 1 fresh lemon
plenty of fresh herbs, such as
   rosemary, bay leaves and thyme
salt and ground black pepper
extra fresh herbs, to garnish

For the sauce

75ml/3fl oz/½ cup light tahini
juice of 1 lemon
1 garlic clove, crushed
45ml/3 tbsp finely chopped fresh
   rosemary

Preheat the oven to 200°C/400°F/Gas 6. Grease the base and sides of a large shallow ovenproof dish or roasting tin.

Slash the fish diagonally on both sides with a sharp knife. Finely crush the coriander seeds and garlic using a pestle and mortar. Mix with the harissa sauce and about 60ml/4 tbsp of the olive oil.

Spread a little of the harissa, coriander and garlic paste inside the cavity of the fish. Spread the remainder over each side of the fish and set aside.

Scatter the tomatoes, onion and preserved or fresh lemon into the prepared dish or tin. (Thinly slice the lemon if using a fresh one). Sprinkle with the remaining oil and season with salt and pepper. Lay the fish on top and tuck plenty of rosemary and other herbs around it. Bake in the oven uncovered, for about 25 minutes, or until the fish has turned opaque – test by piercing the thickest part with a knife.

Meanwhile, make the sauce. Put the tahini, lemon juice, garlic and rosemary in a small saucepan with 120ml/4fl oz/½ cup water and add a little salt and pepper. Cook gently until smooth and heated through. Serve in a separate dish, alongside the baked fish.

Meat Dishes

Rosemary is the perfect herb for flavouring meat.
Lamb and rosemary are an ideal marriage of
flavours as the herb cuts the fattiness of the
meat. Rosemary also balances the richness of
pork and goes well with beef.

ROSEMARY LAMB WITH MUSTARD

Here rosemary is combined with mustard and breadcrumbs to make a crisp coating for rack of lamb.

Serves 6–8

2 or 3 garlic cloves

115g/4oz (about 4 slices) white or
   wholemeal bread, torn into pieces

15ml/1 tbsp rosemary leaves

25ml/1½ tbsp Dijon mustard

30ml/2 tbsp olive oil

3 racks of lamb (7–8 ribs each),
   trimmed of fat, bones
    "French" trimmed

ground black pepper

fresh rosemary sprigs, to garnish

boiled new potatoes, to serve

COOK'S TIP

*This recipe is perfect for
entertaining, allowing you time
with your guests. You can coat
the lamb with the crust before
they arrive and put it in the
oven to cook when you sit
down to eat the first course.*

Preheat the oven to 220°C/425°F/Gas 7.
In a food processor fitted with a metal blade, with the machine running, drop the garlic through the feed tube and process until finely chopped. Add the bread, rosemary, mustard and a little pepper and process until combined, then slowly pour in the oil.

Press the mixture on to the meaty side and ends of the racks of lamb completely covering the surface. Put the racks in a shallow roasting tin and roast for about 25 minutes for medium-rare or 3–5 minutes more for medium (a meat thermometer inserted into the thickest part of the meat should register 57–60°C/135–140°F for medium-rare to medium).

Transfer the meat to a carving board. Cut between the bones into chops. Serve garnished with rosemary and accompanied by boiled new potatoes.

ROSEMARY LAMB CHOP SAUTÉ

When lamb is sautéed with rosemary in a heavy pan, a delicious sauce can be made by deglazing the sediment left behind with a little wine.

Serves 4

675g/1½lb new potatoes

4 lamb chump or loin chops, about
   175g/6oz each

15ml/1 tbsp olive oil

3 fresh rosemary sprigs

75ml/5 tbsp red wine

200ml/7fl oz/scant 1 cup
   chicken stock

5ml/1 tsp cornflour

5ml/1 tsp Dijon mustard

2.5ml/½ tsp black olive paste
   (optional)

10ml/2 tsp white wine vinegar

25g/1oz/2 tbsp unsalted butter

salt and ground black pepper

cooked carrots and petits pois,
   to serve

Bring the potatoes to the boil in a large saucepan of salted water and simmer for 15–20 minutes until tender. Season the lamb with pepper and moisten with oil. Heat a large, heavy-based frying pan over medium heat, add the rosemary and lay the meat over the top. Allow 6–8 minutes for medium-rare or 12–15 minutes for well-done lamb, turning once during the cooking time. Transfer to a warm plate, cover and allow the juices to settle.

Pour any excess oil from the frying pan and discard the rosemary. Return the pan to the heat and heat the sediment until it browns. Add the wine and stir with a flat wooden spoon to loosen, scraping the base of the pan. Pour in the chicken stock and simmer.

Combine the cornflour, mustard and olive paste, if using, in a small bowl, adding 15ml/1 tbsp of cold water to soften. Stir the cornflour mixture into the frying pan and simmer briefly until thickened. Add the vinegar, then stir in the butter. Arrange the potatoes, carrots, petits pois and lamb chops on 4 plates, pour over the sauce and serve.

LAMB WITH ROSEMARY AND MUSTARD

A rosemary and mustard marinade brings a wonderful flavour to this grilled or barbecued lamb.

Serves 6–8

115g/4oz Dijon mustard

1–2 garlic cloves, finely chopped

30ml/2 tbsp olive oil

30ml/2 tbsp lemon juice

30ml/2 tbsp chopped fresh rosemary
* or 15ml/1 tbsp crumbled dried*
* rosemary*

2.25kg/5lb leg of lamb, boned
* and butterflied*

salt and ground black pepper

Combine the mustard, garlic, oil, lemon juice, rosemary, salt and pepper in a shallow glass or ceramic dish. Mix well together.

Add the leg of lamb, secured with skewers, and rub the mustard mixture all over it. Cover the dish and leave the meat to marinate at room temperature for at least 3 hours.

Preheat the grill or light the barbecue. Place the lamb flat on the rack and spread with any mustard mixture left in the dish. If grilling, set the lamb 10–12.5cm/4–5in from the heat. Cook under the grill or over charcoal until the lamb is crusty and golden brown on the outside, 10–15 minutes on each side for rare meat, 20 minutes for medium or 25 minutes for well done.

Transfer the lamb to a carving board and leave to rest for at least 10 minutes before carving into neat, but quite thick slices for serving.

BEEF PLAIT

The attractive plaited pastry encloses a rosemary-flavoured mixture of minced beef, vegetables and cheese.

Serves 4

15ml/1 tbsp oil

450g/1lb/4 cups minced beef

2 leeks, sliced

15ml/1 tbsp tomato purée

15ml/1 tbsp chopped fresh rosemary

25g/1oz/2 tbsp plain flour

150ml/¼ pint/⅔ cup beef stock

450g/1lb prepared shortcrust pastry

flour, for dusting

25g/1oz/2 tbsp freshly grated

   Cheddar cheese

1 egg, beaten

salt and ground black pepper

fresh rosemary sprig, to garnish

new potatoes and French beans,

   to serve

Preheat the oven to 190°C/375°F/Gas 5.

Heat the oil in a large pan, add the minced beef and cook for 5 minutes. Stir in the leeks, tomato purée and fresh rosemary. Season well to taste. Add the flour and cook for 1 minute. Stir in the stock gradually and cook for a further 20 minutes. Allow the mixture to cool.

Roll out the pastry on a lightly floured surface to a rectangle about 30 x 25cm/12 x 10in. Place the minced beef mixture in the centre of the pastry along its length. Top with the grated cheese. Make parallel diagonal cuts either side of the filling, fold in each pastry end and then alternate pastry strips. Brush with beaten egg and bake for 40 minutes until the pastry is golden brown. Garnish and serve with new potatoes and French beans.

ROAST LEG OF LAMB WITH ROSEMARY

Served with haricot or flageolet beans and rich gravy, this French-style roast is a homage to rosemary.

Serves 8–10

2.5–3kg/6–7lb leg of lamb

3 or 4 garlic cloves

olive oil

fresh or dried rosemary leaves

450g/1lb dried haricot or flageolet
beans, soaked overnight in
cold water

1 bay leaf

30ml/2 tbsp red wine

150ml/¼ pint/⅔ cup lamb or
beef stock

25g/1oz/2 tbsp butter

salt and ground black pepper

watercress, to garnish

Preheat the oven to 220°C/425°F/Gas 7. Wipe the leg of lamb with damp kitchen paper and dry the fat covering well. Cut 2 or 3 of the garlic cloves into 10–12 slivers; then, with the tip of a knife, cut 10–12 slits in the lamb and insert the garlic slivers into the slits. Rub with oil, season with salt and pepper and sprinkle with rosemary.

Set the lamb on a rack in a shallow roasting tin and put in the oven. After 15 minutes, reduce the heat to 180°C/350°F/Gas 4 and continue to roast for 1½–1¾ hours (about 18 minutes per 450g/1lb) or until a meat thermometer inserted into the thickest part of the meat registers 57–60°C/135–140°F for medium-rare to medium meat or 66°C/150°F for well-done.

Meanwhile, drain and rinse the beans and put in a saucepan with enough fresh water to cover generously. Add the remaining garlic and the bay leaf, then bring to the boil. Reduce the heat and simmer for 45 minutes–1 hour or until tender.

Transfer the roast to a board and allow to stand, loosely covered, for 10–15 minutes. Skim off the fat from the cooking juices, then add the wine and stock to the roasting tin. Boil over a medium heat, stirring and scraping the base of the tin, until slightly reduced. Strain into a warmed gravy boat.

Drain the beans, discard the bay leaf, then toss the beans with the butter until it melts. Season with salt and pepper. Transfer the lamb to a serving dish, garnish with watercress and serve with the beans and the sauce.

BARBECUED LAMB WITH ROSEMARY

A traditional mixture of parsley, sage, rosemary and thyme – the herbs of the popular folk song – adds a really summery flavour to this simple lamb dish.

Serves 4

1 leg of lamb, about 1.75kg/4½ lb
1 garlic clove, thinly sliced
handful of fresh rosemary
handful of fresh flat leaf parsley
handful of fresh sage
handful of fresh thyme
90ml/6 tbsp dry sherry
60ml/4 tbsp walnut oil
500g/1¼lb medium potatoes
salt and ground black pepper

Place the lamb on a board smooth side downwards, so that you can see where the bone lies. Using a sharp knife, make a long cut through the flesh down to the bone. Scrape away the meat from the bone on both sides, until the bone is completely exposed. Remove the bone and cut away any sinews and excess fat.

Cut through the thickest part of the meat to enable it to open out as flat as possible. Make several cuts in the lamb with a sharp knife, and push slivers of garlic and sprigs of herbs into them.

Place the meat in a bowl and pour over the sherry and oil. Chop about half the remaining herbs and scatter over the meat. Cover and leave to marinate in the refrigerator for at least 30 minutes.

Remove the lamb from the marinade and season. Place on a medium-hot barbecue and cook for 30–35 minutes, turning occasionally and basting with the reserved marinade.

Scrub the potatoes, then cut them in thick slices. Brush them with the marinade and place them around the lamb. Cook for about 15–20 minutes, turning occasionally, until they are golden brown.

COOK'S TIP

If you have a spit-roasting attachment for your barbecue (or oven), the lamb can be rolled with herbs inside, tied securely and spit roasted for 1½ hours. You can cook larger pieces of lamb on the spit.

ROSEMARY AND JUNIPER BEEF STEW

Marinating develops a rich base for casseroles and stews. Here, the complementary flavours of rosemary and juniper berries are dominant.

Serves 4–6

675g/1½lb chuck steak, trimmed
    and cut into 2.5cm/1in cubes

2 carrots, cut into batons

225g/8oz baby onions or shallots

115g/4oz button mushrooms

4 fresh rosemary sprigs

8 juniper berries, lightly crushed

8 black peppercorns, lightly crushed

300ml/½ pint/1¼ cups red wine

30ml/2 tbsp vegetable oil

150ml/¼ pint/²⁄₃ cup stock

30ml/2 tbsp beurre manié

salt

broccoli, to serve

COOK'S TIP

To make beurre manié, combine equal quantities of flour and butter.

Place the meat in a bowl and add the carrots, onions or shallots, mushrooms, rosemary, juniper berries and peppercorns. Pour over the wine, cover and leave in a cool place for 4–5 hours, stirring occasionally.

Remove the meat and vegetables from the bowl with a slotted spoon and set aside. Strain the marinade into a jug.

Preheat the oven to 160°C/325°F/Gas 3. Heat the oil in a frying pan and fry the meat and vegetables in batches until lightly browned. Pour over the reserved marinade and stock and bring to the boil, stirring from time to time. Transfer to a casserole, cover and cook in the oven for 2 hours.

Twenty minutes before the end of cooking stir in the beurre manié, cover again and return to the oven. Season to taste and serve with broccoli.

PROVENÇAL BEEF WITH ROSEMARY

Fish sauces with meat have sometimes been considered odd, but this one works extremely well and is
beautifully balanced by an abundance of rosemary and garlic in the beef marinade.

Serves 4

1.5kg/3lb trimmed fillet of beef
1 large bunch fresh rosemary
4 garlic cloves, crushed
300ml/½ pint/1¼ cups olive oil
salt and ground black pepper
rosemary, to garnish
tomato wedges, to serve

For the tapenade

50g/2oz can anchovies
115g/4oz/1 cup stoned black olives
2 garlic cloves
2 egg yolks
150ml/¼ pint/⅔ cup olive oil
10ml/2 tsp lemon juice

Put the beef in a non-metallic dish and cover with the rosemary, garlic, oil and seasoning. Leave to marinate for at least 2 hours in the refrigerator.

For the tapenade, drain the anchovies and leave them to soak in a bowl of cold water for about 20 minutes. Drain again.

In a food processor fitted with a metal blade, roughly chop the anchovies, olives and garlic cloves. Add the egg yolks and gradually pour in the oil while the blades are still running. Stir in the lemon juice and season to taste. Chill for 30 minutes.

Preheat the oven to 190°C/375°F/Gas 5. Spread the tapenade over the beef and cook in the oven for 45 minutes. Serve sliced with tomato wedges, garnished with rosemary.

HONEY-ROAST PORK WITH ROSEMARY

Rosemary, thyme and honey add flavour and sweetness to pork tenderloin, while mustard brings piquancy.

Serves 4

30ml/2 tbsp clear honey

30ml/2 tbsp Dijon mustard

5ml/1 tsp chopped fresh rosemary

2.5ml/½ tsp chopped fresh thyme

450g/1lb pork tenderloin, trimmed of any fat

1.5ml/¼ tsp pink and green peppercorns, crushed

fresh rosemary and thyme sprigs, to garnish

potato gratin and steamed cauliflower, to serve

For the red onion confit

4 red onions

350ml/12fl oz/1½ cups vegetable stock

15ml/1 tbsp red wine vinegar

15ml/1 tbsp caster sugar

1 garlic clove, crushed

30ml/2 tbsp ruby port

pinch of salt

Preheat the oven to 180°C/350°F/Gas 4. Mix together the honey, mustard, rosemary and thyme in a small bowl. Spread the mixture over the pork and sprinkle with the peppercorns. Place in a non-stick roasting pan and cook in the oven for 35–45 minutes.

For the red onion confit, slice the onions into rings and put them into a heavy-based saucepan. Add the stock, vinegar, sugar and garlic clove, bring to the boil, then reduce the heat. Cover and simmer for 15 minutes.

Uncover the pan, pour in the port and continue to simmer, stirring occasionally, until the onions are soft and the juices thick and syrupy. Season to taste with salt.

Cut the pork into slices and arrange on 4 warmed plates. Serve, garnished with fresh rosemary and thyme sprigs, with the red onion confit, potato gratin and cauliflower.

MARSALA PORK WITH ROSEMARY

Usually used in desserts, here Sicilian marsala partners aromatic rosemary to flavour pork escalopes.

Serves 4

25g/1oz dried cep or porcini
*   mushrooms*
4 pork escalopes
10ml/2 tsp balsamic vinegar
8 garlic cloves
15g/¹⁄₂oz/1 tbsp butter
45ml/3 tbsp marsala
several fresh rosemary sprigs
10 juniper berries, crushed
salt and ground black pepper
cooked noodles and green vegetables,
*   to serve*

COOK'S TIP
Use good-quality pork escalopes
that will not be submerged by
the strong flavour of this
unusual sauce.

Put the dried mushrooms in a bowl and just cover with hot water. Leave to stand.

Brush the pork with 5ml/1 tsp of the vinegar and season with salt and pepper. Put the garlic cloves in a small pan of boiling water and cook for 10 minutes until soft. Drain and set aside.

Melt the butter in a large frying pan. Add the pork and fry quickly until browned on the underside. Turn the meat over and cook for another minute.

Drain the mushrooms in a fine sieve and reserve the soaking liquid. Add the mushrooms and 60ml/4 tbsp of the reserved liquid to the pork, followed by the marsala, rosemary, garlic cloves, juniper berries and remaining vinegar. Simmer gently for about 3 minutes until the pork is cooked through. Season lightly and serve hot with noodles and green vegetables.

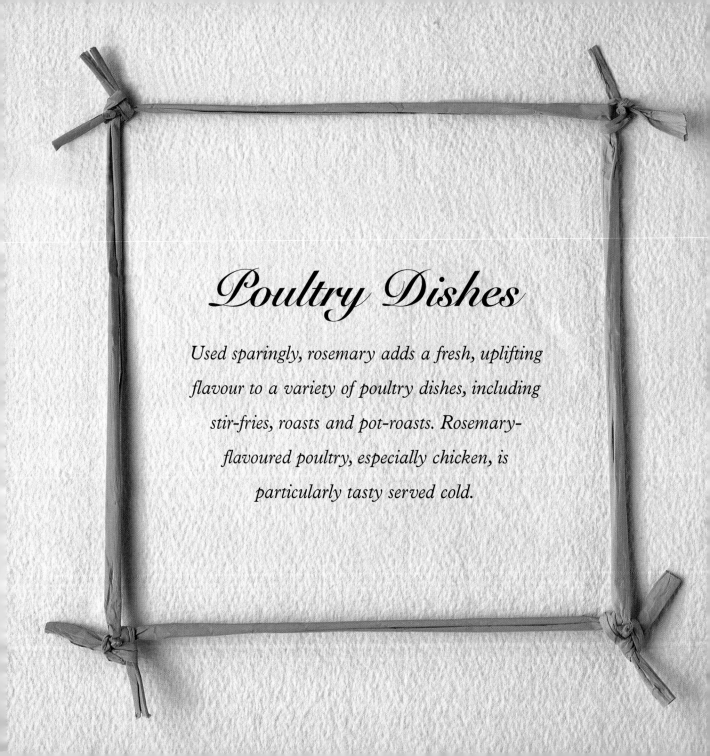

Poultry Dishes

Used sparingly, rosemary adds a fresh, uplifting flavour to a variety of poultry dishes, including stir-fries, roasts and pot-roasts. Rosemary-flavoured poultry, especially chicken, is particularly tasty served cold.

CHICKEN PARCELS WITH ROSEMARY

Rosemary butter is used to moisten tender chicken and to brush the filo pastry enclosing it.

Serves 4

4 chicken breast fillets, skinned

150g/5oz/⅔ cup butter, softened

90ml/6 tbsp chopped fresh rosemary

5ml/1 tsp lemon juice

5 large sheets filo pastry, thawed
*   if frozen*

1 egg, beaten

30ml/2 tbsp grated Parmesan cheese

salt and ground black pepper

COOK'S TIP

This recipe also works well
with turkey breast fillets.

Season the chicken fillets and fry in 25g/1oz/2 tbsp of the butter to seal and brown lightly. Allow to cool.

Preheat the oven to 190°C/375°F/Gas 5. Put the remaining butter, the rosemary, lemon juice and seasoning in a food processor and process until smooth. Melt half the herb butter.

Brush 1 sheet of filo pastry with herb butter. Fold it in half and brush again with butter. Place a chicken fillet about 2.5cm/1in from the top. Dot the chicken with a quarter of the remaining herb butter. Fold in the sides of the pastry, then roll up to enclose the filling completely. Place seam side down on a lightly greased baking sheet. Repeat with the other chicken fillets.

Brush the filo parcels with beaten egg. Cut the last sheet of filo into strips, scrunch and arrange on top. Brush the parcels with the egg glaze, then sprinkle with Parmesan. Bake in the oven for about 35–40 minutes.

CHICKEN LIVER STIR-FRY WITH ROSEMARY

The final sprinkling of lemon, rosemary and garlic gives this quick, easy and inexpensive dish a delightful fresh flavour and wonderful aroma.

Serves 4

500g/1¼ lb chicken livers
75g/3oz/6 tbsp butter
175g/6oz field mushrooms
50g/2oz chanterelle mushrooms
3 cloves of garlic, finely chopped
2 shallots, finely chopped
150ml/¼ pint/⅔ cup medium sherry
3 fresh rosemary sprigs
rind of 1 lemon, cut into thin strips
30ml/2 tbsp chopped fresh rosemary
salt and ground black pepper
flat leaf parsley, to garnish
4 thick slices white toast, to serve

Clean and trim the chicken livers to remove any gristle or muscle. Season them generously with salt and pepper, tossing well to coat thoroughly.

Heat a wok or heavy-based frying pan and add 15g/½oz/1 tbsp of the butter. When it has melted, add the livers in batches (melting more butter where necessary but reserving 25g/1oz/2 tbsp for the vegetables) and flash-fry until golden brown. Drain with a slotted spoon and transfer to a plate, then place in a low oven to keep warm.

Cut the field mushrooms into thick slices and cut the chanterelles in half, depending on their size.

Re-heat the wok or frying pan and add the remaining butter. When it has melted, stir in two-thirds of the chopped garlic and the shallots and stir-fry for 1 minute until golden brown. Stir in the mushrooms and continue to cook for a further 2 minutes.

Add the sherry, bring to the boil and simmer for 2–3 minutes until syrupy. Add 3 rosemary sprigs, salt and pepper and return the livers to the pan. Stir-fry for 1 minute. Sprinkle with a mixture of lemon rind, chopped rosemary and the remaining chopped garlic, garnish with flat leaf parsley and serve with slices of toast.

CHICKEN WITH GARLIC AND ROSEMARY

A sweet wine and garlic sauce coats chicken gently scented with rosemary and thyme.

Serves 8

2kg/4½lb chicken pieces

30ml/2 tbsp olive oil

1 large onion, halved and sliced

3 large garlic bulbs, about 200g/7oz,
  separated into cloves and peeled

150ml/¼ pint/⅔ cup dry white wine

175ml/6fl oz/¾ cup chicken stock

4–5 fresh rosemary sprigs

2 fresh thyme sprigs

1 bay leaf

salt and ground black pepper

COOK'S TIP

Use fresh, new season's garlic if you can find it. There's no need to peel the cloves if the skin is not papery, just remove the outer layer. In France, the cooked garlic cloves are sometimes spread on toasted country bread.

Preheat the oven to 190°C/375°F/Gas 5. Pat the chicken pieces dry with kitchen paper and season with salt and pepper.

Heat the olive oil in a large flameproof casserole and add the chicken pieces in batches, skin side down. Brown over a medium-high heat, turning frequently. Transfer the chicken to a plate.

Add the onion and garlic to the casserole, cover and cook over a medium-low heat until lightly browned, stirring frequently.

Add the wine and bring to the boil; return the chicken to the casserole. Add the stock and herbs and bring back to the boil. Cover and transfer to the oven. Cook for 25 minutes or until the chicken is tender and the juices run clear when the thickest part of the thigh is pierced with a knife.

Remove the chicken pieces from the casserole and strain the cooking liquid. Discard the herbs, transfer the onion and garlic to a food processor and purée until smooth. Skim off any fat from the cooking liquid and discard. Return the cooking liquid to the casserole. Stir in the garlic and onion purée, return the chicken to the casserole and reheat gently for 3–4 minutes before serving.

ROSEMARY POT-ROAST POUSSINS

Pot-roasting in the French manner ensures that poussins, which tend to be rather bland, absorb all the wonderful flavours of young vegetables and fresh rosemary.

Serves 4

15ml/1 tbsp olive oil

1 onion, sliced

1 large garlic clove, sliced

50g/2oz/½ cup diced lightly
    smoked bacon

2 poussins, about 625g/1¼lb each, or
    4 small poussins, about 350g/12oz
    each

30ml/2 tbsp melted butter

2 baby celery hearts, each cut into 4

8 baby carrots

2 small courgettes, cut into chunks

8 small new potatoes

600ml/1 pint/2½ cups chicken stock

150ml/¼ pint/⅔ cup dry white wine

3 fresh rosemary sprigs

1 fresh thyme sprig

1 bay leaf

15ml/1 tbsp butter, softened

15ml/1 tbsp plain flour

salt and ground black pepper

fresh herbs, to garnish

Preheat the oven to 190°C/375°F/Gas 5. Heat the olive oil in a large flameproof casserole and add the onion, garlic and bacon. Sauté for 5–6 minutes until the onion has softened.

Brush the poussins with a little of the melted butter and season well. Lay on top of the onion mixture and arrange the prepared vegetables around them. Pour the chicken stock and wine around the birds and add the herbs.

Cover, bake in the oven for 20 minutes, then remove the lid and brush the birds with the remaining melted butter. Bake for a further 25–30 minutes until golden.

Transfer the poussins to a warmed serving platter. If using larger ones, cut them in half with poultry shears or scissors. Remove the vegetables from the casserole with a draining spoon and arrange them round the birds. Cover with foil and keep warm.

Discard the herbs from the cooking juices. In a bowl mix together the softened butter and flour to form a paste. Bring the liquid in the casserole to the boil and then whisk in teaspoonfuls of the paste until the sauce has thickened. Season the sauce and serve with the poussins and vegetables, garnished with fresh herbs.

ROSEMARY DUCK AND CHESTNUT SAUCE

A sauce of sweet chestnuts complements duck breast that has been steeped in a herb and garlic marinade.

Serves 4–5

several fresh rosemary sprigs
1 garlic clove, thinly sliced
30ml/2 tbsp olive oil
4 duck breasts, boned and fat removed

For the chestnut sauce

450g/1lb chestnuts
5ml/1 tsp oil
350ml/12fl oz/1½ cups milk
1 small onion, finely chopped
1 carrot, finely chopped
1 small bay leaf
30ml/2 tbsp cream, warmed
salt and ground black pepper

COOK'S TIP

The chestnut sauce may be prepared in advance and kept in the refrigerator for up to 2 days. It can also be frozen. Thaw before reheating.

Pull the leaves from 1 rosemary sprig. Combine them with the garlic and oil in a shallow bowl. Pat the duck breasts dry with kitchen paper and brush with the marinade. Allow to stand for at least 2 hours before cooking.

Meanwhile make the chestnut sauce. Preheat the oven to 180°C/350°F/Gas 4. Cut a cross in the flat side of each chestnut with a sharp knife. Place the chestnuts in a baking tin with the oil and shake the pan until the nuts are coated well. Bake in the oven for about 20 minutes. Allow to cool slightly, then peel.

Place the peeled chestnuts in a heavy-based saucepan with the milk, onion, carrot and bay leaf. Cook slowly for about 10–15 minutes until the chestnuts are very tender. Season with salt and pepper. Discard the bay leaf. Press the mixture through a sieve.

Return the sauce to the saucepan. Heat gently while the duck is cooking. Just before serving, stir in the cream. If the sauce is too thick, add a little more cream.

Preheat the grill or prepare a barbecue.

Grill the duck breasts until medium-rare, about 6–8 minutes. The meat should be pink when sliced. Slice into rounds and arrange on warmed plates. Serve with the heated sauce, garnished with the remaining rosemary sprigs.

Vegetable Dishes and Breads

The strong fragrance of rosemary brings to life all sorts of vegetarian dishes and vegetable accompaniments, especially pasta and pulses. It is excellent with mildly flavoured vegetables, as well as tomatoes and peppers.

ROSEMARY ROSTI

Rosemary is an excellent partner for potatoes in this tasty, traditional Swiss dish.

Serves 4

350g/12oz par-cooked potatoes
45ml/3 tbsp olive oil
10ml/2 tsp chopped fresh rosemary
pinch of freshly grated nutmeg
75g/3oz smoked bacon, cut
*   into cubes*
salt flakes and ground black pepper
fresh rosemary sprigs, to garnish
4 quails' eggs, to serve

COOK'S TIP

Serve this dish for a hearty
and warming winter breakfast
or as an unusual starter to a
family meal – hungry, growing
children love it.

Coarsely grate the potatoes and thoroughly pat dry on kitchen paper to remove all the moisture.

Heat a heavy-based frying pan, then add 30ml/2 tbsp of the oil. When the oil is hot, add the potatoes and cook them in batches until crisp and golden. This will take about 10 minutes. Drain them on kitchen paper, mix with the rosemary, nutmeg and plenty of seasoning and keep warm.

Add the bacon to the hot frying pan and stir-fry until crisp. Sprinkle the bacon on top of the potato.

Heat the frying pan again and add the remaining oil. When the oil is hot, fry the quails' eggs for about 2 minutes. Make a pile of the rosemary rosti, garnish with sprigs of fresh rosemary and serve with the eggs.

VEGETABLE CANNELLONI WITH ROSEMARY

A subtle hint of rosemary enhances this milk-flavoured pasta dish, evoking a Mediterranean mood.

Serves 4–6

1 onion, finely chopped

2 garlic cloves, crushed

2 carrots, coarsely grated

2 celery sticks, finely chopped

150ml/¼ pint/⅔ cup vegetable stock

115g/4oz red or green lentils

400g/14oz can chopped tomatoes

30ml/2 tbsp tomato purée

2.5ml/½ tsp ground ginger

5ml/1 tsp chopped fresh rosemary

5ml/1 tsp chopped fresh thyme

40g/1½oz/3 tbsp butter

40g/1½oz/generous 1 tbsp plain flour

600ml/1 pint/2½ cups milk

1 bay leaf

large pinch of grated nutmeg

16–18 cannelloni

25g/1oz Cheddar cheese, grated

25g/1oz Parmesan cheese, grated

25g/1oz fresh white breadcrumbs

salt and ground black pepper

flat leaf parsley, to garnish

To make the filling, put the onion, garlic, carrots and celery into a large saucepan, add half the stock, cover and cook for 5 minutes or until the vegetables are tender.

Add the lentils, chopped tomatoes, tomato purée, ginger, rosemary, thyme and seasoning. Bring to the boil, cover and cook for 20 minutes. Remove the lid and cook for a further 10 minutes until thick and soft. Set aside to cool.

To make the sauce, put the butter, flour, milk and bay leaf into a pan and whisk over the heat until thick and smooth. Season with salt, pepper and nutmeg. Discard the bay leaf.

Fill the uncooked cannelloni by piping the filling into each tube. (It is easiest to hold them upright with one end flat on a board, while piping into the other end.)

Preheat the oven to 180°C/350°F/Gas 4. Spoon half the sauce into the bottom of a 20cm/8in square ovenproof dish. Lay 2 rows of filled cannelloni on top and spoon over the remaining sauce. Scatter over the cheeses and breadcrumbs. Bake in the oven for 30–40 minutes. Grill to brown the top, if necessary. Garnish with flat leaf parsley before serving.

ROSEMARY ROASTIES

These unusual roast potatoes, cooked in their skins, are given an extra lift by the addition of rosemary.

Serves 4

900g/2lb small red potatoes
10ml/2 tsp walnut or sunflower oil
30ml/2 tbsp fresh rosemary leaves
salt and paprika
fresh rosemary sprigs, to garnish

Preheat the oven to 240°C/475°F/Gas 9.
Leave the potatoes whole with the peel on; if large, cut in half. Place the potatoes in a large pan of cold water and bring to the boil. Drain them well.

Drizzle the walnut or sunflower oil over the potatoes and shake the pan to coat them evenly.

Tip the potatoes into a shallow roasting tin. Sprinkle with rosemary, salt and paprika. Roast for 30 minutes or until crisp. Garnish and serve hot.

ROSEMARY AND GARLIC TOASTS

A delicious rosemary-flavoured starter or accompaniment to meat or vegetarian main dishes.

Serves 4

2 whole garlic heads

extra virgin olive oil

fresh rosemary sprigs

1 ciabatta loaf or thick baguette

salt and ground black pepper

Slice the tops off the heads of garlic with a sharp knife. Brush with oil, and then wrap in foil, with a few sprigs of rosemary. Cook on a medium-hot barbecue for 25–30 minutes, turning occasionally, until soft.

Slice the bread and brush generously with oil. Toast on the barbecue until golden, turning once.

Squeeze the garlic cloves from their skins on to the toasts. Chop some rosemary and sprinkle it over the toasts together with a little extra olive oil and salt and pepper to taste.

COOK'S TIP

Roast a few slices of aubergine, pepper and onion over the barbecue to spread over the toasts for variety.

ROSEMARY AND SEA-SALT FOCACCIA

Focaccia is an Italian soft, flat bread made with olive oil. Here it is given added flavour with fresh rosemary and a sprinkling of coarse sea salt.

Makes 1 loaf

350g/12oz/3 cups plain flour
2.5ml/½ tsp salt
10g/¼oz/2 tsp easy-blend dried yeast
about 250ml/8fl oz/1 cup
  lukewarm water
45ml/3 tbsp olive oil
1 small red onion
leaves from 1 large fresh
  rosemary sprig
5ml/1 tsp coarse sea salt

Sift the flour and salt into a large mixing bowl. Stir in the yeast, then make a well in the centre of the dry ingredients. Pour in the water and 30ml/2 tbsp of the oil. Mix well, adding a little more water if the mixture seems dry.

Turn the dough on to a lightly floured surface and knead for about 10 minutes until smooth and elastic.

Place the dough in a greased bowl, cover and leave in a warm place for about 1 hour until doubled in size. Knock back and knead the dough for 2–3 minutes.

Roll out the dough to a large circle, about 1cm/½in thick, and transfer to a greased baking sheet. Brush with the remaining oil.

Halve the onion and slice into thin wedges. Sprinkle the onion over the dough, with the rosemary and sea salt, pressing in lightly.

Using a finger, make deep indentations in the dough. Cover the surface with greased clear film, then leave to rise in a warm place for 30 minutes.

Meanwhile, preheat the oven to 220°C/425°F/Gas 7. Remove the clear film from the dough and bake the loaf in the oven for 25–30 minutes until golden. Serve warm.

ROSEMARY BREAD

Sliced thickly, this rosemary bread is delicious with cheese or soup for a light lunch or supper.

Makes 1 loaf

10g/¼oz/2 tsp easy-blend dried yeast
175g/6oz/1½ cups wholemeal flour
175g/6oz/1½ cups self-raising flour
25g/1oz/2 tbsp butter, plus extra
    for greasing
50ml/2fl oz/¼ cup warm water
    (45°C/110°F)
250ml/8fl oz/1 cup milk (room
    temperature)
15ml/1 tbsp sugar
15ml/1 tbsp salt
15ml/1 tbsp sesame seeds
15ml/1 tbsp dried chopped onion
15ml/1 tbsp fresh rosemary leaves,
    plus extra to decorate
115g/4oz/1 cup diced
    Cheddar cheese
coarse salt, to decorate

Mix the yeast with the flours in a large mixing bowl. Melt the butter. Stir the warm water, milk, sugar, butter, salt, sesame seeds, onion and rosemary into the flour mixture. Knead thoroughly until quite smooth.

Flatten the dough, then add the diced cheese. Quickly knead it in until it has been thoroughly incorporated.

Place the dough in a clean bowl greased with a little butter, turning it so that it becomes greased on all sides. Cover with a clean, dry cloth. Put it in a warm place and leave for about 1½ hours until the dough has risen and doubled in size.

Grease a 23 x 13cm/9 x 5in loaf tin with the remaining butter. Knock back the dough to remove some of the air, and shape it into a loaf. Put the loaf into the tin, cover with the clean cloth used earlier and leave for about 1 hour until doubled in size once again. Preheat the oven to 190°C/375°F/Gas 5.

Bake the loaf in the oven for 30 minutes. During the last 5–10 minutes of baking, cover with foil to prevent it from becoming too dark. Remove from the tin and leave to cool on a wire rack. Decorate with rosemary leaves and coarse salt scattered on top.

ROSEMARY BEAN PURÉE WITH RADICCHIO

The slightly bitter flavours of radicchio and chicory make a wonderful marriage with the creamy and aromatic rosemary-flavoured bean purée.

Serves 4

400g/14oz can cannellini beans

45ml/3 tbsp low-fat fromage blanc

finely grated rind of ½ large orange

juice of 1 large orange

15ml/1 tbsp finely chopped fresh
    rosemary

4 heads chicory

2 medium radicchio

15ml/1 tbsp walnut oil

strips of orange rind, to garnish

COOK'S TIP

Other types of beans, such as haricot, mung and broad beans, could also be used.

Drain the beans, rinse and drain again. Purée the beans in a blender or food processor with the fromage blanc, grated orange rind, orange juice and rosemary. Set aside.

Cut the chicory in half lengthways. Cut each radicchio into 8 wedges.

Lay the chicory and radicchio on a baking tray and brush with walnut oil. Grill for 2–3 minutes. Serve with the purée and scatter over the strips of orange rind.

ROSEMARY BAKED PEPPERS

Make sure that there is a basket of freshly baked warm bread at hand so that none of the delicious rosemary-flavoured juices from this dish are wasted.

Serves 8

2 red peppers

2 yellow peppers

1 red onion, sliced

2 garlic cloves, halved

6 plum tomatoes, quartered

50g/1oz/½ cup black olives

5ml/1 tsp soft light brown sugar

45ml/3 tbsp sherry

3–4 fresh rosemary sprigs

30ml/2 tbsp olive oil

salt and ground black pepper

COOK'S TIP

You could use 4 or 5 well-flavoured beefsteak tomatoes instead of plum tomatoes if you prefer. In this case, cut them into thick wedges instead of into quarters.

Preheat the oven to 200°C/400°F/Gas 6. Seed and core the red and yellow peppers, then cut each into 12 strips. Place the peppers, onion, garlic, tomatoes and olives in a large roasting tin. Sprinkle over the sugar, then pour over the sherry. Season well, cover with foil and bake in the oven for 45 minutes.

Remove the foil from the tin and stir the mixture well. Add the rosemary sprigs. Drizzle over the olive oil. Return the tin to the oven for a further 30 minutes until the vegetables are tender. Serve hot.

POTATO, ROSEMARY AND GARLIC PIZZA

New potatoes, smoked mozzarella, rosemary and garlic make the flavour of this pizza unique.

Serves 2–3

350g/12oz new potatoes

45ml/3 tbsp olive oil

2 garlic cloves, crushed

1 pizza base, 25–30cm/10–12in
*   in diameter*

1 red onion, thinly sliced

150g/5oz smoked mozzarella
*   cheese, grated*

10ml/2 tsp chopped fresh rosemary

salt and ground black pepper

30ml/2 tbsp freshly grated Parmesan
*   cheese, to garnish*

Preheat the oven to 220°C/425°F/Gas 7. Cook the potatoes in boiling salted water for 5 minutes. Drain well. When cool, peel and slice thinly.

Heat 30ml/2 tbsp of the oil in a frying pan. Add the sliced potatoes and garlic and fry for 5–8 minutes until the potatoes are tender.

Brush the pizza base with the remaining oil. Scatter over the onion, then arrange the potatoes on top. Sprinkle with the mozzarella and rosemary. Grind over plenty of black pepper and bake in the oven for 15–20 minutes until crisp and golden. Remove from the oven and sprinkle with the Parmesan before serving.

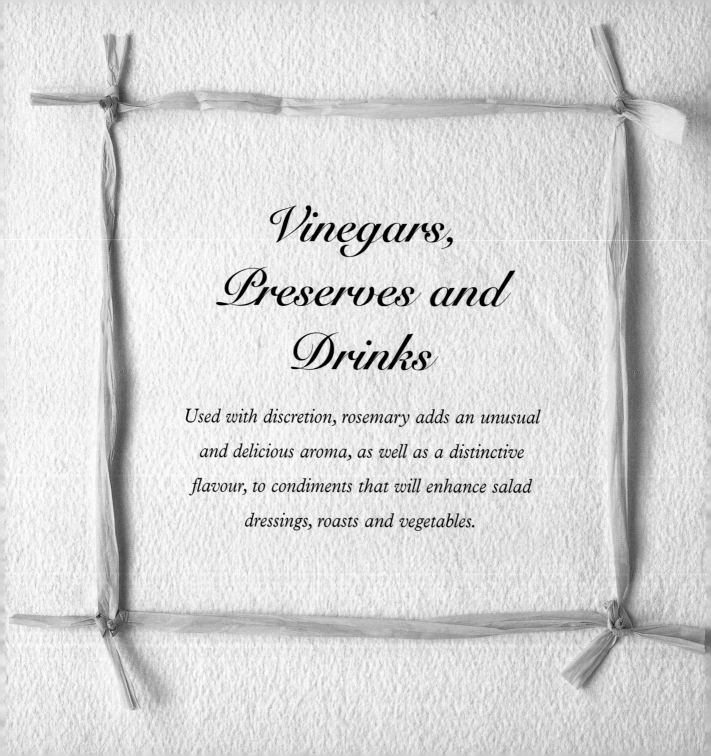

Vinegars, Preserves and Drinks

Used with discretion, rosemary adds an unusual and delicious aroma, as well as a distinctive flavour, to condiments that will enhance salad dressings, roasts and vegetables.

ROSEMARY VINEGAR

This easy-to-make rosemary-flavoured vinegar will turn an ordinary salad dressing into something special. It also makes an attractive and welcome, home-made present for gourmet friends.

Makes about 600ml/1 pint/2½ cups
fresh rosemary sprigs to fill a
  600ml/1 pint/2½ cup measure,
  plus extra to decorate
600ml/1 pint/2½ cups white distilled
  vinegar

COOK'S TIP
You could also use white wine or cider vinegar instead of distilled vinegar.

Fill a sterilized, wide-necked bottle or jar with the sprigs of rosemary. Fill to the top with vinegar. Cover tightly and place in a sunny position for 4–6 weeks.

Filter the vinegar mixture through a coffee filter paper. Discard the rosemary. Heat the vinegar until it begins to simmer, but do not boil.

Wash the bottle or jar and its lid well in hot, soapy water, rinse thoroughly and dry in a warm oven. Pour the vinegar back into it or into other sterilized, decorative bottles. You can add a fresh sprig or two of rosemary for decorative purposes if you wish, then seal and label. Store in a dark place. Use within 1 year.

MARINATED OLIVES WITH ROSEMARY

The addition of rosemary enlivens these scrumptious marinated olives, which make irresistible nibbles for serving with pre-dinner drinks.

Serves 4

225g/8oz/1⅓ cups unstoned
    green olives
3 garlic cloves
5ml/1 tsp coriander seeds
2 small red chillies
2–3 thick slices of lemon, cut
    into pieces
1 large fresh rosemary sprig
75ml/5 tbsp white wine vinegar

COOK'S TIP
For a change, use a mix of caraway and cumin seeds in place of the coriander and mix black and green olives.

Spread out the olives and garlic on a chopping board. Using a rolling pin, crack and flatten them slightly. Crack the coriander seeds in a mortar with a pestle.

Mix the olives, garlic, coriander seeds, chillies, lemon pieces, rosemary sprig and wine vinegar in a large bowl. Toss well, then transfer the mixture to a clean glass jar. Pour in water to cover. Store in the refrigerator for at least 5 days (preferably 10 days) before serving. Serve at room temperature.

HERBAL PUNCH

A good party drink with more than a hint of rosemary that will have people coming back for more, this punch is a delightful non-alcoholic choice for drivers.

Serves 30 plus

450ml/¾ pint/2 cups clear honey

4 litres/7 pints/17 cups water

450ml/¾ pint/2 cups freshly squeezed
    lemon juice

45ml/3 tbsp fresh rosemary leaves,
    plus extra to decorate

1.5kg/3½lb/8 cups sliced strawberries

450ml/¾ pint/2 cups freshly squeezed
    lime juice

1.75 litres/3 pints/8 cups sparkling
    mineral water

ice cubes

3–4 scented geranium or strawberry
    leaves, to decorate

Combine the honey, 1 litre/1¾ pints/4¼ cups water, one-eighth of the lemon juice, and the rosemary leaves in a saucepan. Bring to the boil, stirring until all the honey is dissolved. Remove from the heat and allow to stand for about 5 minutes. Strain into a large punch bowl.

Press the strawberries through a fine sieve into the punch bowl, add the rest of the water and lemon juice and the lime juice and sparkling mineral water. Stir gently. Add the ice cubes minutes before serving and float the geranium or strawberry leaves and extra rosemary leaves on the surface.

Yogurt Cheese with Rosemary

These little spheres of cheese flavoured with rosemary, thyme and chilli are bottled in olive oil.

Makes about 900g/2lb

750g/1¾lb Greek sheep's yogurt

2.5ml/½ tsp salt

10ml/2 tsp crushed dried chillies or
chilli powder

15ml/1 tbsp chopped fresh rosemary

15ml/1 tbsp chopped fresh thyme
or oregano

about 300ml/½ pint/1¼ cups olive
oil, preferably garlic-flavoured

Sterilize a 30cm/12in square of muslin by steeping it in boiling water. Drain and lay over a large plate. Mix the yogurt with the salt and tip on to the centre of the muslin. Bring up the sides of the muslin and tie firmly with string.

Hang the bag on a kitchen cupboard handle or in a suitable position where it can be suspended with a bowl underneath to catch the whey. Leave for 2–3 days until the yogurt stops dripping.

Sterilize 2 x 450g/1lb glass preserving or jam jars by heating them in the oven at 150°C/300°F/Gas 2 for 15 minutes.

Mix together the chilli and herbs. Take teaspoonfuls of the cheese and roll into balls with your hands. Lower into the jars, sprinkling each layer with the herb mixture. Pour the oil over the cheese until completely covered. Store in the refrigerator for up to 3 weeks.

To serve the cheese, spoon out of the jars with a little of the flavoured olive oil and spread on to lightly toasted bread.

Cook's Tip

If your kitchen is particularly warm, find a cooler place to suspend the cheese. Alternatively, drain the cheese in the refrigerator, suspending the bag from one of the shelves and with a bowl underneath.

RED PEPPER AND ROSEMARY JELLY

Whole sprigs of fresh rosemary are suspended in this wonderful amber-coloured jelly.

Makes 1.75kg/4lb

450g/1lb tomatoes, chopped

4 red peppers, seeded and chopped

2 red chillies, seeded and chopped

fresh rosemary sprigs

300ml/½ pint/1¼ cups water

300ml/½ pint/1¼ cups red
  wine vinegar

2.5ml/½ tsp salt

900g/2lb/4½ cups preserving sugar
  with added pectin

250ml/8fl oz/1 cup liquid pectin

Place the tomatoes, peppers, chillies, a few rosemary sprigs and the water in a stainless-steel saucepan and bring to the boil. Cover and simmer for 1 hour or until the peppers are tender and pulpy.

Suspend a jelly bag and place a bowl underneath. Sterilize the jelly bag by pouring through boiling water. Discard the water and replace the bowl.

Pour the contents of the saucepan slowly into the jelly bag. Allow the juices to drip through slowly for several hours but do not squeeze the bag or the jelly will become cloudy. Sterilize the jars and lids required.

Place the juice in a clean saucepan with the vinegar, salt and sugar. Discard the pulp in the jelly bag. Heat the juice gently, stirring occasionally, until the sugar has dissolved. Boil rapidly for 3 minutes.

Remove the saucepan from the heat and stir in the liquid pectin. Skim the surface with a piece of kitchen paper to remove any foam.

Pour the liquid into the sterilized jars and add a sprig of rosemary to each jar. Place a waxed disc on the surface of each and seal with a lid of cellophane paper and an elastic band. Allow to cool, then label and decorate with ribbons. Store in a cool place.

INDEX